How to Achieve Your Goals

Lessons from Alexander the Great

Tirath S Gill

Leadership Lessons of Alexander Great

Are you still to learn that the end and perfection of our victories is to avoid the vices and infirmities of those whom we subdue?

How to Achieve Your Goals

Copyright: 2013 Tirath S Gill

All rights reserved

Printed in the United States of America

Leadership Lessons of Alexander Great

Dedicated to

NPS Cheema

APS Cheema

Acknowledgments

Mr. NPS Cheema and his son Amritpal Singh Cheema were beloved family members that departed for their heavenly abode during the last year. This book is dedicated to their memories. They were true gentlemen and noble in spirit. I am also very appreciative of the wisdom of my father Major Raghbir Singh Gill. My son Savy humored me by discussing some of the ideas. I am grateful to him for his objective feedback.

Introduction

There are a number of books on Alexander the Great and his story is recounted with every generation.

In this book are defined key traits of Alexander that made him such a phenomenal success.

One may legitimately ask why we should study an ancient king when times were so different. In response, I would offer that he is worth studying because human behavior has not changed that much over the last two thousand years and the methods he used to motivate others are still applicable today.

As a singular human being, he is truly unique. He not only possessed the physical courage of a lion, but a penetrating mind that mastered the art of leading men and achieving great goals.

One of his most useful abilities was the ability to speak well and paint with words a vision for his people. He set before his people a clear goal of world conquest and actually made good on his promises. He led

How to Achieve Your Goals

his armies as an unstoppable juggernaut that rolled for 13,000 miles. In a short span of 13 years between the ages of 20 and 33, he had conquered almost 90% of the known world.

Historians marvel that he never lost a battle and defeated armies more than twice the size of his own forces. His achievements in fact are so astonishing that many believed at the time that he possessed supernatural powers. In Egypt, he was worshipped as a deity by some and inspires a cult-like awe and amazement even today.

For all of the above reasons, we should study his successes. Having said the above, it is worth pointing out that he also had magnificent flaws. These are also singled out in this book as we can learn from his mistakes as well.

I hope this book will help you believe in your own ability to achieve great goals.

TSG

Leadership Lessons of Alexander Great

Note

The lessons do not have a chronological significance. All are equally important and work with each other. They can be read in any order and organized as you see fit.

On the use of the pronouns he and she, the pronoun he is often used for convenience. These lessons are equally applicable to both men and women.

Lastly, this book is for educational purposes only and is not meant as a substitute for professional advice or counsel

How to Achieve Your Goals

Contents

Lesson: Live an Examined Life 15

Take away Points: 16

Lesson: Turn a Crisis into an Inspiration 19

Take Away Points 19

1. Seek inspiration and motivation from a higher power. Many great leaders have been inspired by such experiences. 19

Lesson: Have Great Role Models. 21

Actionable steps: 22

Lesson: Renew Yourself Daily 23

Life of Alexander: 23

Actionable Points: 23

Lesson: Have Supreme Self-confidence . 25

Background: 25

Modern examples: 26

Take Away Points 27

Lesson: Learn, Relearn and Practice Often 30

Background: 30

Actionable Steps: 31

Lesson: Remain Incurably Hopeful 33

Actionable points: 34

Lesson: Set Lofty Goals 36

Leadership Lessons of Alexander Great

Background: 36
Take Away Points 36
Modern day examples of Lofty Goal Setting: 38
    Lesson: Be Audacious 40
Life of Alexander the Great: 40
Actionable Points: 42
    Lesson: Be Persistent and Break Big Jobs into Small Jobs 43
Background: 43
Actionable steps 44
    Lesson: Set Deadlines 45
Background: 45
Actionable Points: 46
    Lesson: Think out of the box 47
Actionable Points: 47
    Lesson: Be willing to challenge conventional wisdom 49
Actionable Points 49
    Lesson: Avoid alcohol - If used, avoid use in excess 51
Background: 51
Actionable Steps 52
    Lesson: Control Your Anger 54

How to Achieve Your Goals

Background: 54
Take Away Points 55
   Lesson: Let them think you can fly 57
Background: 57
Modern Day Examples: 59
Actionable Points: 60
   Lesson: Bury the Elephants 61
Background: 61
Actionable steps 63
Background: 64
Actionable Steps 64
   Lesson: Be faster 66
Background: 66
Actionable Steps 67
   Lesson: Use the cutting edge of Technology 68
Background: 68
Actionable Points 69
   Lesson: Use local guides 71
Background: 71
Actionable Points: 71
   Lesson: Invite Ideas 73
Background: 73

Leadership Lessons of Alexander Great

Actionable Plan: 73
   Lesson: Combine Data 75
Actionable Points: 75
   Lesson: Allow for rest 77
Background: 77
Actionable Points 78
   Lesson: Be Sensitive to Local Customs .. 79
Background 79
Actionable Points 80
   Lesson: Get the Most Able and Intelligent People 81
Background 81
Actionable points 83
   Lesson: Care about Your People 84
Actionable points 85
   Lesson: Be Loyal and Value Loyalty 88
Life of Alexander the Great: 88
Take Away Points: 89
   1. Be loyal and value loyalty 89
   2. Reward talent and loyalty in front of others 89
   Lesson: Honor Love 90
Life of Alexander the Great: 90

How to Achieve Your Goals

Philanthropic Couples: 90
Actionable points 91
   Lesson: Take Security Seriously 93
Life of Alexander: 93
Modern Hazards 95
Actionable Points 95
   Repeated Lesson: Be Democratic Whenever Possible 96
Take Away Points: 97
   Lesson: Burn your Wagons 98
Modern Day Examples: 99
Actionable Steps: 100
   Lesson: Multitask Intelligently 102
Modern Day Examples: 102
Actionable Steps: 104
   Lesson: Master Logistics and Organization 105
Modern Day Examples: 106
Actionable Steps 106
   Lesson: Timing is Everything 107
Modern Day Examples: 110
Actionable Steps: 110
   Lesson: Build Alliances 112

Actionable Plan 114
   Lesson: Honor your parents/forgive them for any wrongs and move on 116
Background: 116
Actionable Points: 119
   Lesson: Plan for your succession 121
Take Away Points: 122
   References 123
   Epilogue.. 125

Lesson: Live an Examined Life

Alexander the Great was a restless soul. He did a great deal of soul searching and was always in search for greater meaning in his life. This is evident by his moodiness at times with his friends and his teachers.

He was an inquisitive student and delved into the practical and the philosophical aspects of warfare.

During his short life, he made continuous attempts to attain a deeper spiritual and existential awareness, and sometimes went out of his way to consult with an oracle or a seer. His search helped him to overcome doubts and contributed to his single-mindedness of purpose.

Alexander in his quest for self-knowledge did find validation and inspiration from a prophetess that he believed spoke with the inspiration of a higher power. She proclaimed to him, "My son, you are invincible". He believed in her and indeed never lost a battle in his lengthy campaign.

His self-examination gave him a bearing and a compass for the rest of his life.

Take away Points:
1. Take steps to become more self-aware of what you want out of life. Take the time to consider for yourself what you would be willing to fight for and what sacred values you will defend to your death. By clarifying your core values, you will avoid much meaningless meandering.
2. Make a plan of action for reaching your goals. Define in a sentence or two the guiding vision and reason for your goals.
3. Be willing to adapt and be patient as long as you are keeping with the grand goal.

How to Achieve Your Goals

4. Learn to persevere even if you feel like you are not making progress as long as you are moving towards the guiding vision.

5. By knowing yourself, you will have achieved a key source for energy and drive that is lacking in those who are not sure of what they want in life. When you know who you are, your inner self and your outer goals will find a natural alignment.

6. Knowing yourself always takes a bit of work and can cause anxiety. Once you go through the anxiety, you will be stronger for having confronted the anxiety.

7. It is helpful to find a special place of your own where you can relax, meditate, and ask yourself honest questions.

8. Books and biographies are a great resource for gathering ideas as they were for Alexander the Great.

9. Sometimes a book can reveal much that can be life changing.

10. Explore other avenues to self-discovery. This can include a talk with a priest, pastor, Rabbi, Guru or mentor. Make your

enquiries simple and straight from the heart.

11. Write down the above somewhere and refer to it on a regular basis to course correct if your actions are not in keeping with your vision.

Socrates proclaimed that the unexamined life is not worth living. He felt it was no different than the life of an animal who only knows the instinctual purposes of needing food shelter and sex without any perceptions of a higher purpose. Chanakya, a famous Indian philosopher and sage from the same era had a very similar opinion as well.

How to Achieve Your Goals

Lesson: Turn a Crisis into an Inspiration

Alexander the Great appears to have had an incredible experience during his exile to Epirus after the falling out with his father. After their reconciliation, he seems to have attained a certain maturity, drive and focus that he had not possessed before.

Take Away Points

1. Seek inspiration and motivation from a higher power. Many great leaders have been inspired by such experiences.
2. It is important to do this especially when the chips are down. Crisis has a way of mobilizing our spiritual and inspirational reserves.
3. Many go through what St. John called the dark night of the soul to arrive at a crystallization of God's purpose for them.
4. Many political leaders have arrived at their higher truths and motivation during periods of deprivation, exile or imprisonment.
5. Remember that there will always be setbacks. Do not despair however. To use

Leadership Lessons of Alexander Great

a football analogy, half time scores are meaningless. It is not over until the fourth quarter is over. Second half comebacks and fourth quarter miracles abound in life.

How to Achieve Your Goals

Lesson: Have Great Role Models.

Alexander had many eminent warrior role models to choose from. His greatest role model was Achilles, a hero of the Iliad. Achilles personified for him all that a noble warrior should be, fearless in vengeance, generous in victory and modest in his ways. Alexander the Great, like his role model, strived to achieve historic conquests while maintaining his chivalry and modest ways. Like Achilles, Alexander too

Leadership Lessons of Alexander Great

showed temperance, treated worthy opponents well, and was generous beyond belief. With those that resisted him, he could inflict withering punishment and humiliation.

The other role model was his father, King Philip. The Macedonian king was a gifted general who strengthened his country by making innovations to the Macedonian army. These included the refinement of the infantry phalanx formations and an improvement in their weapons and shields. Phillip was also the first to create a full time professional army. His troops were housed in barracks and drilled on a regular basis to keep them proficient and battle ready. Alexander learned the importance of being prepared and of being innovative from his father.

Actionable steps:

1. Find a role model and emulate the values that they hold. The role model can be from the past or present. He or she can be a religious figure, a family member or a leader that you admire.

2. Read biographies of significant people and learn from their successes and their failures. Emulate the positive qualities that made them a success and incorporate these gradually into the pattern of your own approach. If it improves

How to Achieve Your Goals

your functioning, then keep it. If it does not help, then go forward and pick another trait of a leader that you admire and see how that works for you. Leadership and skill at leading people is a lifelong effort. You get better over time.

Leadership Lessons of Alexander Great

Lesson: Renew Yourself Daily

Life of Alexander:

Alexander had a routine to center himself that he followed on most days. He would offer prayers and make the ritual sacrifices to the Gods that he admired. He also read the Greek Classics for pleasure and inspiration. He was fond of hunting and took to it when he found time.

Actionable Points:

1. Find an activity that renews your spirits and sense of purpose. It may be an activity such as exercise, fishing, hunting, or physical sports. It may also be time with family, watching a great movie, prayer, reading, travelling or quiet contemplation.

2. Do this on a regular basis to keep your bearings and your motivation alive. Take time to review your progress and rededicate

How to Achieve Your Goals

yourself to your vision and the goals you set for yourself during your self-examination.

Leadership Lessons of Alexander Great

Lesson: Have Supreme Self-confidence

Background:

Alexander the Great had immense confidence in his own abilities. He was also able to inspire confidence in others through his speeches and conversations. In battle, his confidence was supreme and spread to all those under his command.

He was never in doubt about the outcome of any battle. The night before the epic battle at Gaugamela, his generals were amazed that he slept more soundly during the night than ever before.

He also conveyed his confidence and sense of certain victory by leading his troops from the front. The sight of their young king leading the charge worked to inspire and arouse the fighting spirit of his troops. His soldiers had total confidence in him because of his confidence in himself.

How to Achieve Your Goals

Modern examples:

The ability to have confidence in oneself and inspire this in others is an important hallmark of those that are truly great.

The modern day cult figure Steve Jobs had this reputation.

Those who worked with him say that he had the ability through sheer willpower to bend reality to his vision and others would find themselves irretrievably drawn into his projects, no matter how impractical they may have seemed to them at first.

The beloved four-time president FDR displayed a similar level of confidence. He had immense faith in himself and in the nation that he lead through the dark years of depression and later World War II.

He conveyed this to the American public through his famous weekly fireside chats broadcast over the radio. His confidence allowed people to believe in the future again and climb out of the misery and poverty of their times.

Winston Churchill also displayed a crazy level of self-confidence and was able to rally Great Britain through the darkest days of World War II when London was under the constant air attacks of Nazi Germany.

Leadership Lessons of Alexander Great

Mahatma Gandhi had an immense faith in himself. His faith arose from his religious convictions and ethical fortitude, which told him that injustice cannot stand against the combined will of millions engaged in nonviolent protests. His confidence gave many Indian freedom fighters the courage to brave the batons and guns of British troops during their nonviolent protests. Although the role of the militant Indian leaders cannot be understated, Mahatma was the key figure in mobilizing world opinion favorably to the Indian Independence movement. He was proclaimed the father of the nation when India gained independence in 1947. It has become an independent republic and is now the largest democracy in the world.

Take Away Points

1. Be self-confident and focused, especially during moments of crisis.
2. Lead from the front. Be willing to lead by example if needed.
3. If you suffer from a lack of self-confidence, it may be related to abuse and deprivation in the past.
4. There are several things you can do to overcome this.
5. First, see if your lack of confidence is related to a realistic appraisal of the challenges you face. If this is the case,

How to Achieve Your Goals

delegate this to someone else who has more experience in dealing with the problem.

6. If the lack of self-confidence is pervasive, then consider getting psychotherapy, or a psychiatric evaluation to rule out depression, and a medical examination to ascertain that you are physically healthy and not suffering from a physical problem or hormonal anomalies.
7. Depression can be treated very effectively by a good psychiatrist without causing sideeffects.
8. Individual therapies vary in their effectiveness. Cognitive Behavioral Therapy is very helpful.
9. Communication skills courses taught by Scientology Centers and Auditing can be helpful for many people. They have earned a bad reputation due to some loonies in their organization but the courses that they offer are very useful.
10. If you can find acceptance by God or an adopted religion that does not exploit you, you should allow God to grant you the love and acceptance that you may not have experienced in your life. Such a giving over to God and praying to him on a personal level has utterly transformed many people's lives. Born-again Christians are a good example and many have been able to repair their lives and

totally turn it around for the better with their newfound faith. The love of God and acceptance can be a great redeemer indeed.

11. Once you achieve some success, do not forget it or minimize it. Use it to bolster your self-confidence for now and the future. Do not let go of your self-confidence no matter what challenges come your way.

12. Don't let temporary setbacks affect your self-confidence. Be willing to wait and make a strategic retreat but remain true to your long-term goals and your ability to achieve these.
13. Remember that confident people will ask for other people's opinion and delegate tasks to them. Do not think that you have to do everything on your own.
14. Dedicate a scheduled time to improving your speaking skills, even if your think you are a good speaker. Public speaking and the ability to give extemporaneous talks is an important skill for a leader and can always be improved. Consider joining toastmasters or a similar organization to hone your ability to use the spoken word.

How to Achieve Your Goals

Lesson: Learn, Relearn and Practice Often

Background:

Alexander had a great teacher in Aristotle. Aristotle, in addition to being very erudite, was also a brilliant and insightful teacher.

He understood that knowledge was most reliably gained by hands-on experience. He taught his students with a mix of didactic lectures and practical exercises.

As an example, he would set up combat games for his young students with a hypothetical battlefield on a simulated terrain. Sometimes he would include bizarre and unusual obstacle to the usual strategy to make the students think on their feet. He would let them learn to work out a creative strategy and compliment or critique the solutions offered. With unstated intent, he also taught them with these exercises to collaborate and rely on each other's reasoning and skills.

He stressed the importance of pooling ideas and working together. He also instructed his pupils to be open to revising plans as new information came to light.

Leadership Lessons of Alexander Great

Aristotle made them practice their war craft until it became second nature to Alexander and his companions.

Later on in his campaigns, Alexander did come across many unusual and challenging scenarios. His readiness to adapt to new situations was a lesson he had learned well from Aristotle. His dexterity with battle plans would lead to spectacular successes in the battles at Granicus, Issus, Gaugamela and on the river Hydaspes. The strategies used by Alexander were remarkable for their ingenuity and cunning.

In fact, they are still the subject of study by many military academies.

The brilliant tactics and refined use of human psychology are the things of legend and have rightly earned him the moniker of being called "The Great". His brilliance is a thing to behold even in the faceless modern warfare of smart bombs and drones.

Actionable Steps:

1. When you are searching for a school for your chosen vocation, find out what practical hands-on experience is provided.
2. Part of being a good leader is being a good teacher. When you are trying to

How to Achieve Your Goals

teach or coach someone, be sure to give them examples and have them practice what you teach them. To further consolidate the knowledge, have them teach it to another employee. Be patient, kind and encouraging when you are in the coaching mode of being a leader.
3. Look to see if others who are working in the field would be willing to mentor you.
4. Whenever possible, make an effort to get hands-on experience in the field.
5. One of the goals of getting practical experience is to learn to think on your feet. Practicing the application of your skills will improve your ability to be successful in the real world.
6. Remember that knowledge without the ability to apply it is of little value. Learn to use what you learn in many situations as possible.

Leadership Lessons of Alexander Great

Lesson: Remain Incurably Hopeful

Alexander the Great almost emptied his personal estates in order to provide pensions for the families of his commanders. When one of his generals asked him what he had kept for himself, Alexander replied that he had kept his hopes. Upon hearing this, some of his generals declined his generous offers and vowed to be soldiers of hope alongside him.

Alexander would sometimes make a daring strategic decision in the middle of some of his big battles. He used initiative, speed and courage to turn the tide of the war. Some of these battles could have easily gone the other way but his hope in his calculated risks paid off in a big way on more than several occasions.

Julius Caesar, who admired Alexander immensely, also took many hopeful and calculated risks during his conquest of Gaul for the Roman Empire. He also took calculated gambles based on hope in his political career and these paid off as well for him.

Napoleon Bonaparte was another acolyte of Alexander the Great. He also used initiative, took calculated risks and defeated armies much bigger than his own. If he had settled into a

How to Achieve Your Goals

conventional battle plan, he may not have become the Emperor over so much of Europe.

Actionable points:

1. When an opportunity presents itself, one should be willing to take hopeful calculated risks even if all of the information is not available.
2. A person should be prepared to seize the opportunity when it presents itself. Fortune and luck favors the prepared mind.
3. Setbacks can be a blessing. Failure should not be seen as a failure but as a learning opportunity. A leader should learn from the failure so as to succeed the next time around. He should use a setback to consider innovative approaches to the problem that may have been overlooked before.
4. A leader should remind himself and his troops of their past successes and not become hopeless or dismayed due to temporary setbacks.
5. There is no such thing as absolute security. The search for absolute security may prevent one from taking necessary actions.

6. One should allow hope and a clear vision to drive him towards the attainment of a predetermined goal. A leader should not be enslaved by unreasonable fear that cages him into mediocrity.

How to Achieve Your Goals

Lesson: Set Lofty Goals

Background:

Alexander set lofty goals and had the unique ability to convince others that these were achievable.

When his father died, there were immediate uprising in the north and to the south of Greece. He quickly subdued these and after being named the leader of the Greeks, put before them the lofty goal of defeating the great Persian Empire that had ruled them for several hundred years.

The grandeur and loftiness of this goal is hard to overstate. A more practical king would have been content to rule over his kingdom and deemed the prospect of such an invasion as foolishly lofty. That, however, was exactly what Alexander did and the rest as they say is history.

Take Away Points
1. The act of setting great goals is important for a leader.

Leadership Lessons of Alexander Great

2. He must be willing to challenge the limits of what is considered achievable.
3. Write down a goal that you feel is lofty and "unrealistic"
4. Make a determination to achieve that goal
5. Write down resources required to achieve that goal
6. Try to get others to collaborate with you when possible.
7. Work in a diligent and focused manner towards your goals and ignore the naysayers.

How to Achieve Your Goals

Modern day examples of Lofty Goal Setting:

Sometimes a leader needs to set lofty and distant goals. As an example, John F. Kennedy set a goal for America in the early 60s to send a man to the moon and safely bring him back before the end of the decade. At the time, it seemed like an unreasonable goal as America was behind in the space race and some missions had ended disastrously. Once the goal was set however, the country rose to the challenge and did put man on the moon in 1969

Smallpox disease was a global terror that killed, maimed and blinded millions of people. The World Health Organization set a goal for the eradication of this illness. It was deemed to be a lofty goal and perhaps unattainable. After this lofty goal was set however, nations came together in vaccination campaigns and the World Health Organization declared the disease eradicated in 1980.

When Ted Turner dreamed of a 24-hour cable news network, some considered the plan lofty and harebrained. He persisted however and history has proven him magnificently correct. The 24-hour cable news network or CNN is now

Leadership Lessons of Alexander Great

a fixture in the lives of millions of people around the globe who rely on it for the latest breaking news.

How to Achieve Your Goals

Lesson: Be Audacious

Life of Alexander the Great:
Alexander came across many difficulties during his career.

During the early part of a campaign, he was told that trying to cross the Granicus river with its tall banks was foolish. His generals told him that it was impossible because the enemy would have the advantage of spearing Macedonian troops that tried to climb up the banks. It was late in the afternoon and the din of armor clanging and confusion of differing advice challenged the young king's decision-making. Alexander decided to order the attack that very evening, despite the seemingly difficult odds.

As recounted by historians, the sun began to set and was in the eyes of the Persian troops on the east bank. The Macedonian troops, with Alexander at the head of the charge were able to break through and gain a foothold on the opposite bank. His legendary phalanxes were also able to cross. The enemy was no match for the 12 foot sarissa spears and soon the center of the enemy ranks was on its heels and turned to run. This was the first big victory for Alexander on Persian soil and greatly increased his esteem in the eyes of his soldiers and countrymen. If Alexander had listened to the litany of the pessimists, the course of human history may have been very different.

As his armies marched deeper into the Persian Empire, Darius met them at the battle of Issus, near the seacoast of modern-day Syria. Darius had much greater strength in numbers and everyone thought that the odds were once again against Alexander.

Due to his audacity of charging after Darius when the opportunity presented itself, the tide of the battle turned. This battle resulted in a stunning victory, during which Darius narrowly escaped with his life.

How to Achieve Your Goals

With this victory, Alexander's army gained enormous wealth and treasure. Some valuable royal hostages were also captured. These included the mother of the emperor, his wife and two daughters. They were abandoned by the Persian army as the soldiers scrambled to save their own lives.

To his great credit, Alexander treated his royal hostages with honor and afforded them all the privilege that was standard for royalty in those days.

At the epic battle of Gaugamela again, he took the initiative and chose the time of the battle.

The forces of Darius III were huge in number again and arrayed on a vast and seemingly limitless battlefield. There were those who told him that such a battle was heavily lopsided and could not be won. Alexander, however, crafted a brilliant strategy and defeated Darius.

Actionable Points:
1. Just when the odds seem the longest, be audacious, kindle hope and be encouraging to others. Make an objective assessment and figure out a unique way for success. If you look hard enough for a way to succeed, you will find it.

Leadership Lessons of Alexander Great

2. Discount the naysayers and nihilists and minimize their influence upon you and others.
3. Periodically remind your people of the vision and give them a sense of their progress.

How to Achieve Your Goals

Lesson: Be Persistent and Break Big Jobs into Small Jobs

Background:

Alexander fixed his goals and objectives after careful analysis and foresight and did not budge from those goals until he had succeeded. Once he began, he used amazing speed, initiative and tenacity in achieving his goals. One can see this in his conquest of Tyre, where he built a bridge almost a kilometer into the sea to connect the island to the mainland. He persisted despite several setbacks and sabotages by the enemy all the while modifying his plans and adjusting his strategy, but not relenting on his goal.

There was much work to be done and he delegated tasks to different teams. Some gathered the stones that were available nearby and started to build the mole. He delegated tasks to other generals to mobilize the navy of Phoenicians to provide support. He undertook attacks on both sides of the island and delegated the tasks to different sets of soldiers, some more proficient than others.

Leadership Lessons of Alexander Great

Through a coordination of many different elements, subdivision of tasks, and persistence, Alexander the Great was able to take Tyre.

The conquest of Tyre was a historic victory that spread Alexander's fame far and wide. After he consolidated his hold on Tyre, he effectively neutralized the Persian navy so that it was never again a threat to him on the coast of his newly conquered lands in the Middle East.

Actionable steps

1. Break down the tasks that need to be done in order to attain your goal.
2. Break the big tasks into smaller subtasks and delegate those subtasks to others when possible.
3. You must expect that there will be some hurdles.
4. You should help your efforts by removing these hurdles and distractions whenever possible.
5. Do not give up on a worthy goal because of any level of setbacks.

How to Achieve Your Goals

Lesson: Set Deadlines

Background:

Alexander had an instinct for timing and dictated that certain tasks be accomplished by a certain time. This drove his army to accomplish marches and building projects that others thought were miraculous. The very act of setting a clear objective and setting a deadline has the force of mobilizing the human will and concentrating effort towards achievement of the goal.

The benefit of setting deadlines is well stated by Cyril Parkinson of the Parkinson law fame. Simply stated, it makes the following assertion:

"Work expands so as to fill the time available for its completion. "

This means that if you give a person two weeks to finish a task, he or she will take two weeks to accomplish most of the task. If you give the person two months, most of the work will remain undone until the two months are about up.

Leadership Lessons of Alexander Great

Actionable Points:

1. Set daily goals and deadlines for yourself and others
2. Keep one list of things to do instead of multiple lists
3. Give specific assignments to specific individuals instead of to a group. Authorize that individual to deputize others as needed but the final responsibility should remain his or hers.
4. Create an environment that provides the least amount of interruptions for completion of the task.
5. Reward those that achieve their goals and do a good job. This can be simple as verbal praise in public.

How to Achieve Your Goals

Lesson: Think out of the box

In the battle with Porus, the war elephants were a terror to the horses and the men. Alexander was able to neutralize this threat by attacking the mahouts or the elephant drivers and the sensitive parts of the animals with arrows and spears. This had the effect of panicking the elephants and causing them to turn on their own men in retreat.

As his own horses were not used to fighting with elephants, he approached the battle with his cavalry on the flanks of the battle lines and captured the horses of Porus that could ride near the elephants and used these in the battle as they came into his possession.

When there was a challenge from Tyre or the residents of the Sogdian Rock, he came up with innovative solutions to overcome the hurdles posed on his path.

Actionable Points:

1. Be ingenious and restate the problem that you are facing. Not every battle

has to be engaged on the battlefield chosen by the adversary.
2. Break down the problem into subcomponents and see which problem is the root problem. Look at the problem from different perspectives
3. Think out of the box, look beyond the conventional approaches.
4. Ask for suggestions, brainstorm with others, and be willing to welcome all ideas no matter how zany or strange.
5. See how the problem can be turned into an advantage. Look at parallel situations that have occurred in other contexts and study how these were resolved.

Lesson: Be willing to challenge conventional wisdom

Alexander challenged many of the conventional beliefs by approaching them with creativity. He conquered passes vulnerable to sabotage by asking his soldiers to join their shields above them to provide cover from stones hurled from above. He solved the problem of the isolation of Tyre from the mainland by building a bridge to it. Others said the bridge could not be built. He neutralized the Persian navy that others thought could not be defeated by cutting it off from fresh water supplies. He challenged conventional wisdom of not crossing certain rivers when they were flooded by building rafts of skin hides stuffed with straw. In short, he achieved great objectives *because* he challenged conventional wisdom.

Actionable Points
1. Sometimes you have to question conventional wisdom when you are told

that a certain objective cannot be achieved.
2. You may have to be creative and put in an extraordinary effort in order to achieve a worthwhile goal. This may be the equivalent of building a bridge over an ocean, but you must be willing to put in the effort if needed.
3. You must be willing to persevere despite setbacks and never lose your faith in your ability to accomplish what you have set yourself to do.

How to Achieve Your Goals

Lesson: Avoid alcohol - If used, avoid use in excess

Background:

Alexander the Great was quite sober and moderate in his habits in the beginning. With time however, he began drinking on a regular basis. His drinking was facilitated by the obligatory banquets where Macedonian leaders were expected to drink and dine with their troops.

Alexander participated in this with dutiful debauchery and fell prey to the devious trap of regular alcohol use. The following applied well to Alexander and his liquor.

"At first the man takes the drink, then the drink takes a drink, then the drink takes the man"

At first, Alexander the Great was moderate in his drinking and he only drank on social occasions. Gradually however, his drinking bouts became more frequent and longer. In due time, he became tolerant and resorted to drinking more heavily. In the later years, it began to affect his judgment.

The burning of Persepolis during a drunken bout was cause for much regret in him and indicates a behavior that was out of control and cause for much grief.

He became more self-absorbed, suspicious and given to rashness that was in contrast to his more studied and modest approach of earlier times.

In a drunken rage, he killed his friend Cleitus. In his growing suspiciousness, he also killed Calisthenes, his appointed historian and two of his able generals Philotus and the father of Philotus, the legendary and much respected general Parmenion.

Actionable Steps
1. Avoid the regular use of alcohol. When alcohol is used, it should be used in moderation and never to excess.
2. In addition to the well-know effects of killing liver cells and scarring the liver with fibrous cirrhosis, alcohol also effects the heart, brain and the intestines. There is malabsorption of essential nutrients that leads to physical and psychological effects.

How to Achieve Your Goals

3. While the physical damage of chronic alcoholism is more obvious, the psychological effects are underrecognized but just as damaging.
4. These can include severe depressive states, paranoia and jealous delusions with retaliatory aggressive behaviors.
5. If there is a family history of alcohol related problems, you may have a genetic vulnerability to alcoholism. In this case, one should be extra careful and consider total abstinence from alcohol.

Leadership Lessons of Alexander Great

Lesson: Control Your Anger

Background:

Although in the beginning Alexander showed moderation and had good control over his anger, he struggled with anger in the later years. Some of this can be attributed to the stress caused by witnessing carnage on a grand scale.

One of the most infamous episodes of uncontrolled anger is an incident wherein he speared and killed his friend Cleitus, a soldier of legendary valor. This soldier had saved Alexander's life at the battle of Granicus, cutting down an opponent that was about to strike Alexander with a raised sword.

Apparently, an argument had erupted with the outspoken Cleitus. Some of the soldiers separated the two men. Cleitus however came back into the tent and began to argue loudly with Alexander again. At this point, Alexander flew into a rage and grabbed his spear and thrust it into Cleitus. He saw his lifelong friend crumble to the ground and die at his feet.

How to Achieve Your Goals

Alexander the Great was so upset by the event that he did not come out of his tent for three days. He was kept under watch by his generals so that he may not take his own life in sorrow and guilt.

He soon got over this but continued to have problems with his anger from time to time. He also lost some trust and respect amongst his troops after this show of lack of control over his anger.

Take Away Points

1. Do not give in to your anger. An act of violence resulting in injury or death can never be taken back.
2. Do not give into your rage no matter what the precipitating action or cause maybe. Letting anger control you is proof that you have been overcome and outsmarted by the circumstances or person creating the rage.
3. People may manipulate and control you if they know that you cannot handle your anger.
4. If it is something to be angry about, do it in the right way.
5. The correct way is to open a dialogue with the person who is causing it and ask them to desist from the behavior and explain what your grievance is.

6. If the other person is intoxicated, it is wise to talk to them only when they are sober.
7. If the cause of the conflict cannot be resolved easily, it is better to disagree agreeably and limit further contact.
8. An approach through a mediator maybe possible later on.

Lesson: Let them think you can fly

Background:

During his conquests in the eastern part of the Persian Empire, he came to a hill top fortress called the Sogdian rock. It lay in modern Tajikistan north of Afghanistan, and its occupants were battle-hardened warriors who felt their abode was impregnable. They felt totally secure in their sky dome and rebuffed the offers of Alexander for a peaceful surrender. The hill tribesmen were so confident of their secure location that they taunted Alexander by saying that he would only reach them if he could make his men fly. Alexander was the wrong person for them to challenge.

Whenever challenged, Alexander rose to the challenge. He was known to solve enigmatic problems through creativity and ingenuity. He lived up to this reputation this time again. He knew that among his troops were men from the mountainous areas of Macedonia that were good climbers.

He appealed to their warrior spirit by stating that challenge that had been laid by the

Leadership Lessons of Alexander Great

Sogdian chieftains. He asked for volunteers and provided additional motivation by providing an additional stipend to those that volunteered.

Listening to Alexander appeal to their valor and with the offer of an additional financial reward, a few hundred of his mountaineers came forward and offered their services.

At the chosen time, he ordered his "flying men" to start the climb. They climbed through the darkness and although some men fell to their death, most of them made it to the top of the rock.

At the chosen time while he hid his army from view, he ordered his few hundred men to unfurl their flag above the camp where the enemy was encamped.

When the Sogdians saw the Macedonian troops atop them from the unexpected side with their flag unfurled, and not seeing any troops below because Alexander had hidden them, they thought that Alexander had miraculously scaled the sheer cliffs with his whole army during the night.

They were overwhelmed by the audacity of such a climb. They reasoned that he was not someone they could fight as he seemed to have the powers of a God and willingly surrendered to his troops.

How to Achieve Your Goals

Alexander let them believe that he indeed could make men fly and accepted their surrender.

Modern Day Examples:

When General Schwarzkopf encircled the entire Iraqi army from a direction they least expected, they were truly awed by the speed of the campaign led by armored divisions that travelled hundreds of miles in the dark of the night with night vision technology and satellite directed paths. His approach of encircling the Iraqi army from behind was a tactical advantage that decided the outcome of the battle.

When the announcement calling for their surrender of the enemy troops was made, the hungry and isolated soldiers who had planned to brave a frontal assault realized that they had been outmaneuvered and capitulated en mass.

General Schwarzkopf is modest about claiming credit but his exploits in the first Gulf war were no less than those of Alexander. It is not surprising that Alexander the Great was a subject of admiration and study for General Schwarzkopf as well.

Leadership Lessons of Alexander Great

Actionable Points:
1. Rise to the challenge and use your ingenuity and intelligence to overcome obstacles in your path.
2. Let your reputation stand and do not diminish the perception of your abilities and prowess.
3. It will avoid unnecessary challenges in the future if others know that you will not be one to give up in the face of resistance.
4. Harness the power of volunteers and diverse talents among your people. Use volunteers to take on challenging tasks. Make clear the rewards that will be available for the successful completion of the tasks.
5. Outsource to as wide a net as possible, even if it is outside of your organization if the task is important and needs to be done well. Let the doors be open to the all talent from anywhere.

How to Achieve Your Goals

Lesson: Bury the Elephants

Background:

In the battle with Porus, Alexander the Great faced a true conundrum.

Horses have a natural fear of elephants. The elephants' scent is enough to drive them away. The natural tendency of even trained warhorses was to run away.

The most feared and effective force that Alexander had was his cavalry battalions. Alexander relied heavily on his cavalry for speed, maneuverability and shock value and not being able to use his cavalry in the familiar manner posed a real dilemma.

He himself rode with the cavalry in every battle and had led both the charges against Darius that had turned the tide of previous battles at Issus and Guagamela.

His adversary King Porus also knew this and realized that Alexander's horses were not desensitized and would not charge at the elephants. He accordingly interspersed the elephants along the length of his formations.

Leadership Lessons of Alexander Great

Alexander the Great resolved this problem by recognizing that he could not make a head long charge at the ranks of his opponent.

He orchestrated a complex plan to lull his opponent into complacency and then used the ruse of a rainy night to take half his forces upstream about 15 miles for a crossing. The plan used elements of misdirection, and psychology of desensitization for decreasing vigilance.

He had his soldiers march in formations up and down the river, get drunk and disorderly in the evenings and give the impression of the force being disorganized and full of clowns that may not be serious fighters.

On the chosen time of attack during a dark and stormy night, he kept half of his troops stationed at the main base and ordered them to continue the same ruse. He instructed them to light the same number of campfires, simulate the same disorderly behaviors and even had one of the men parade around in Alexander's outfit pretending to be him.

He took the remainder of the force with him, left half of it at a midpoint and took the remainder to a point further up the river. The small garrison that was stationed there had one elephant. When they crossed over, his infantry overtook the garrison, they killed that elephant and buried it to get rid of the smell. He then

How to Achieve Your Goals

ordered his cavalry horses to cross over from the other side. Getting rid of that one elephant allowed him to get his horses across the river and ultimately to his victory.

The rest of the battle was a string of brilliant maneuvers, directing the rest of his troops to cross over from the midway point as he marched down from the other side. He also deployed his newly formed light infantry comprised mostly of the Bactrian horsemen with great effect.

Actionable steps

Recognize the elephants in your organization. These are the individuals that drive away good people from your organization and scare others from joining you.

They are often domineering, have an exaggerated perception of themselves and focus on being mercilessly critical of others.

If there are domineering negative people in your organization that are lowering the morale of others, counsel them to correct their behaviors.

If it does not work, consider letting them go.

Get rid of the elephants.

Leadership Lessons of Alexander Great

Lesson: Lead from the front

Background:

Alexander always led from the front. This inspired his troops to give their utmost in order to gain the approval and praise of their commander. It gave them courage to take the risks that their own king was taking. It also earned him the respect of his troops when they saw his boldness and valor in the most dangerous parts of the battle. Alexander also

How to Achieve Your Goals

believed that the courage the commander displays has a direct role in the outcome of any battle.

He is said to have remarked, "I am not afraid of an army of lions if they are led by a sheep but am worried if it is an army of sheep lead by a lion"

Actionable Steps
1. Never ask anyone to do something you yourself are not willing to do.
2. Take initiative in important events. Provide your presence during important discussions and deliberations where the course of a company or an organization is to be discussed.

Leadership Lessons of Alexander Great

Lesson: Be faster

Background:

Alexander the Great led one of the fastest armies. He marched his armies up to 40 miles a day while normal armies in those days marched 25 miles at their very best.

His speed and agility caught many of his enemies off guard and gave him a tactical advantage. He surprised his enemies by often arriving before the enemy spies could get there.

He achieved his speed by lightening the load each soldier carried. He also made innovative changes to how the divisions were organized. Lastly, the men were well supplied and well fed due to his mastery of logistics.

He chose generals for their speed in battle. One of his generals Ptolemy was known for his speed and Alexander used him to capture the rebel Bessus. As Bessus retreated further into the hinterlands, the relentless fast paced pursuit of Ptolemy led to the followers of Bessus deserting him and offering him up to the Greeks in order to escape their own persecution.

How to Achieve Your Goals

During the uprising in Thebes soon after his ascension to the throne, Alexander marched at full speed to arrive at the gates of the city-state, much to the chagrin of the residents who thought he was weeks, if not months away. His speed in arriving to put down the rebellion convinced the other city-states to unite under his banner instead of meeting the same fate as Thebes, whose residents paid a heavy price for their insurrection.

Actionable Steps
1. Act as soon as possible on matters that require your attention
2. Delegate tasks to others who are known for their speed if you cannot get to it right away
3. Know the expected date of completion and try it to get it done before the deadline every time.

Leadership Lessons of Alexander Great

Lesson: Use the cutting edge of Technology

ALEXANDER ADAPTS

Background:
Alexander was a scholar at heart and studied the new cultures and new military technology of lands that he conquered. When he saw a new method of warfare that

How to Achieve Your Goals

was effective, he adopted it or improved upon it. His father was the same way and made improvements to the length of the spears or the "sarissa" when he saw the Thebans use their longer spears to great effect. The Macedonian army also improved on the design of the shields by making them lighter and hanging from the neck of the soldier. It could be easily shifted to the right or the left depending on the side from where the enemy might attack a phalanx. The belt contained a device also that made the carrying of the spear easier.

During his conquest of Bactria, he learned of the effective guerillas tactics and their hit and run tactics from horseback. He recruited a division of these soldiers and used them with utmost effectiveness in the battle with Porus.

There are modern day examples of technology deciding the crucial battles of our times.

In World War II, the use of advanced weapons was a significant factor in the success of Hitler's armies.

Leadership Lessons of Alexander Great

Later on, the development of more advanced technologies by the Allies such as the radar changed the tide of the war again.

The Japanese army was fearless and almost unstoppable until the American army came up with a superior technology that harnessed the energy of the atom. The use of the atomic bomb was the sole factor that convinced the Emperor of Japan to offer an unconditional surrender.

Actionable Points
1. Be the first or among the first to adopt a new technology that helps you reach your goals faster.
2. When possible, innovate and amend current technology to make it better even if it is a small improvement.
3. Keep your innovations protected and unique as long as possible.
4. Hire people that have an aptitude for learning new technologies and commission them to scour the field for bringing new ideas to the organization.
5. Train your people in new technology and have them use it on a regular basis to get proficient with its effective use.

How to Achieve Your Goals

Lesson: Use local guides

Background:

On more than one occasion, Alexander the Great relied on local guides to lead his entire armies to safe exits and to strategic battlefield advantage.

He was a shrewd student of human behaviors and could read a face like a book. He was good at detecting when someone was lying and when they were reliable informants.

He utilized this skill to gain valuable knowledge about the local terrain and secret routes.

He used large rewards that he knew would gather fame as inducements for other reliable guides to offer their services.

Actionable Points:
1. Talk to the locals and use their experience and knowledge to build upon on your other knowledge base.
2. Ask the locals about the problems they experience and how they resolve these.

3. Ask them about what their difficulties are and what would make their lives easier.
4. Be sincere in rewarding useful information and offer confidentiality and protection if needed.

How to Achieve Your Goals

Lesson: Invite Ideas

ALEXANDER INVITES IDEAS

Background:

Alexander shared the Greek ideas of democracy and asked the opinions from others.

Alexander the Great was legendary for having brainstorming sessions with his generals that sometimes went late into the night.

Leadership Lessons of Alexander Great

All were allowed to voice their ideas without fear of criticism.

Alexander was able to pick out the brightest ideas and incorporate them into the strategic battle plans.

Because of the democratic process, his generals also felt vested in making the plan succeed.

Actionable Plan:
1. Promote open discussion and the sharing of ideas between your people and yourself. Keep an open door policy.
2. Provide an anonymous tip line. Use this to improve things, not go after people.
3. Set up offices so that there are common areas of congregation around the water cooler or a break room where coffee, tea or other refreshments are provided. Have conference rooms readily available and make them available without booking
4. Present a problem to the group and ask them to volunteer ideas on an anonymous tip line if they choose to use that avenue.

Remember that most people like to have their opinion considered. They look on it favorably and it is not time consuming as it might appear.

Lesson: Combine Data

Alexander the Great created a unique system of gathering and analyzing data that is still used by the CIA, KGB and other secret service agencies. It involves gathering of data from multiple data streams, analysis from different experts and others to synthesize the different data and make predictions that are useful for planning purposes. Alexander had experts on his campaign who specialized in different cultures, the geology of different terrains, mapmakers, botanists, seers and prognosticators. He did not give overwhelming credence to any one source alone but used his own instincts along with the combined data to make his decisions.

On more than one occasion, his campaign was able to surprise the enemy due to logistical insights that he had gained from his refined intelligence analysis.

Actionable Points:

1. Gather intelligence from different sources but do not give too much emphasis to any one source.

Leadership Lessons of Alexander Great

2. Merge the data gathered.
3. Value human intelligence and intuition
4. Assess the value of specialized information and use it if it to your advantage.
5. Use historical and geographic intelligence if it is relevant to the situation.
6. Study others who have tackled similar problems and use the knowledge of their experience to refine your own plans.
7. Learn from the success and failure of others.
8. Protect your data sources. Honor confidentiality if asked for.
9. Use models to understand data if needed.

How to Achieve Your Goals

THEY MARCHED WITH HIM TO THE ENDS OF THE EARTH

Leadership Lessons of Alexander Great

Lesson: Allow for rest

Background:

Alexander had an instinctive understanding of the psychological need of human beings to rest, feel appreciated and to celebrate success.

He allowed such opportunities for his army. This allowed his men to adjust psychologically to the new lands they conquered.

He also allowed them liberal leave to go home if needed and did not coerce soldiers to stay on the campaign if they were emotionally exhausted or wanted to go home for personal reasons.

Before launching a campaign, he provided them a clear plan and reason for the next battle plan. His men bought into this plans readily and were willing warriors eager to do heroic acts and feats of valor to earn reputation, reward and fame that Alexander promised.

When needed, he knew how to get them out of the dormant resting phase and launch them into new campaigns with renewed vigor.

During difficult campaigns, Alexander knew the power of a hot meal and was the first to

How to Achieve Your Goals

recognize that an army marched on its stomach. After a cold night on a mountain before the battle of Issus, Alexander ordered that each man be served a hot meal on the morning of the battle as the fog lifted from the valley below.

He gave one of his famous motivational speeches laying out the noble reasons for the Macedonian cause versus the hired mercenaries and slave soldiers of the opposing camp of Darius.

The meal and the rousing speech was enough to lift their spirits. His army went on to win the battle of Issus that practically gave Alexander control of the modern day Middle East.

Actionable Points

1. Celebrate success and important milestones.
2. Reward and recognize important achievements.
3. Put things in perspective and explain the rewards of future projects and victories.
4. Frame the struggle from the perspective of the strengths of your camp vs. their future challenges.

Lesson: Be Sensitive to Local Customs

Background

Alexander was a cultured and educated warrior king.

He was appreciative of works of creativity and art when he saw them.

He was also conscious of the cultural sensitivities of the people that he conquered. He tried to participate in their rites and rituals in order to win their hearts and minds.

He put effort into learning the cultures of the people he conquered. He would find out when their festivals occurred and would pay homage to their Gods and their customs.

He did not desecrate their temples and did not disrespect the temple priests.

He forbade the desecration of places of worship and publically punished those that he found had done so.

How to Achieve Your Goals

His tolerance of other faiths speaks of a refined intellect that was able to appreciate the good in others faiths even when it was not his own culture or faith. His acts were not political shows but borne of a genuine sensitivity and good will. He engaged in this policy in the face of strong opposition from many of his own soldiers.

These acts won him favor amongst the nations he ruled.

Actionable Points

1. Do not ever discriminate based on a person's ethnicity, color, sex or any other distinguishing features. Judge men and women based on talent and virtue alone.
2. Allow different persons to practice their faith and relationship with a higher power in their own way.

Leadership Lessons of Alexander Great

Lesson: Get the Most Able and Intelligent People

Background

Alexander had some of the ablest generals. He chose them carefully and was a good judge of talent and men. He retained the most successful generals from his father's army and used their experience and judgment at key and critical junctures.

Some of his generals such as Hephastian, Ptolemy and Seleucid had been his classmates at the academy with Aristotle as their common teacher. He had played many a war game with them when they were young and they could almost read each other's minds.

They knew each other's talents and abilities and there was a feeling of mutual respect and brotherhood amongst them. All were very talented and loyal to Alexander.

Many of them put their own life at risk in order to save Alexander's life in the thick of many a battle. Alexander understood each one's

How to Achieve Your Goals

strengths and used these abilities for different purposes.

He knew Hephastian excelled at dealing in a diplomatic manner and he used him to forge alliances with the Persians even before Persia had been conquered.

Some historians believe that his secret alliances may have been of some help in the victory over Darius and subsequent consolidation of the empire under Alexander's rule. He was able to secure a truce with many tribes without the need for bloodshed.

General Ptolemy was legendary for his speed and Alexander put him at the head of his light infantry. Alexander sent him in pursuit of the Bactrian rebel Bessus, who had proclaimed himself successor to Darius. As expected, Ptolemy was able to overtake and capture Bessus ahead of Alexander's arrival.

Ptolemy was also an able administrator and after Alexander's death, became the Pharaoh of Egypt. His dynasty lasted for several generations, ending in the death of Queen Cleopatra.

Actionable points

1. Hire the best talent and the most intelligent individuals. Even if they're not familiar with the exact type of work that you are doing, they will be more easily trainable and may come up with innovative ideas in the future.

2. Look for history of past achievements or flashes of talent when choosing leaders.

3. Look for sincerity and a willingness to learn.

4. Avoid people that have a history of repeated failures.

How to Achieve Your Goals

Lesson: Care about Your People

Historians have opined that Alexander knew the names of 10,000 soldiers and their particular family backgrounds. He knew of their past exploits and their valorous deeds. He would bring these up to remind them of their accomplishments when they were facing difficult battles.

He knew their particular tribal backgrounds and the area of the country where they came from. He knew the internecine rivalries that existed amongst some of them. He would use these to strategically locate them on the battlefield.

After the battle was won, he would visit the wounded troops and encourage them with the news of the victory and the brave deeds of their compatriots.

After the campfires were lit, the soldiers would begin the storytelling and the recounting of heroic acts from the battle of the day and of battles past. Alexander was fond of participating in these long talks and of hearing his people speak about themselves. They appreciated the fact that their king was there to share in their trials and triumphs.

Leadership Lessons of Alexander Great

Modern day examples: The most successful generals like Eisenhower and Monty visited with their troops. The best CEOs go to the work line and meet with the blue-collar workers to share their stories and listen to their circumstances. They do this even when there are no photo opportunities. They participate in an occasional picnic or birthday party of the ground troops, not because it looks good but because they genuinely care and want to experience the life of the worker. This has the effect of creating a family atmosphere and closeness amongst the ranks.

Actionable points

1. If you want people to follow you and help you achieve your goals, take the time to listen to them and their day-to-day heroics and hurdles. Celebrate them and celebrate with them. This concern should not be mere theatrics but be out of genuine goodwill. When possible, the leader should reward good work. He or she should also recognize special and unique situations that require special assistance. He should make an honest effort to provide such help.
2. When possible, the leader should spend time with his workers so they feel accepted and appreciated. He should also

How to Achieve Your Goals

recognize their anxieties and their unstated needs for security. An attempt should be made by the effective leader to understand the concerns and anxieties of his people. He or she should then try to address these in whatever reasonable way possible. Open communication and willingness to work together will go a long way even if all the problems cannot be solved. More importantly, it will help to create genuine goodwill that can be useful for the future. The good will earned by a genuine compassionate leader is never wasted. It will help him in many ways seen and unseen.

3. When workers feel appreciated by their leader, they will give that little extra, which can take a product or a job from good to great. The Jesuits have a word for it: Magis. They inculcate it in their priests to give something extra for God in all their efforts. This added something shows up in their stellar achievements in many different fields.
4. Ask your people to give you that something extra, reward them for it, and they will not let you down. Earn their goodwill and appeal to the nobler virtue and lasting satisfaction of a job well done.
5. The above steps seem simple, but are of immense importance. The people's goodwill is a resource that is tapped by

Leadership Lessons of Alexander Great

great leaders and ignored by those destined for mediocrity.

Lesson: Be Loyal and Value Loyalty

Life of Alexander the Great: Alexander prized loyalty above all else. He was loyal to his soldiers and suffered their pain and difficulty in every battle. He showed this by being at the side of his soldiers, tending to their wounds when they were injured and never asking them to do what he would not do himself.

Leadership Lessons of Alexander Great

He would be the first to charge into battle and his body bore many a battle scar. Even though some of these injuries could have been life threatening, he never stopped leading from the front. Alexander asked his soldiers to recount their exploits at their campfires and applauded them in front of others for their heroic feats.

Even if the stories were exaggerated, he played along. He recognized that the telling of such tales would lead others to perform acts of valor and heroism. The soldiers that exhibited loyalty and those that acted with courage were rewarded in public. By rewarding and recognizing their loyalty, he earned the undying love of his troops. They would have marched to the ends of the earth for him. As a matter of fact, they actually did march behind him to the outer limits of the known world.

Take Away Points:

1. Be loyal and value loyalty.

2. Reward talent and loyalty in front of others

How to Achieve Your Goals

Lesson: Honor Love

Roxanna

After conquering the tribes of Sogdia and the Sogdian rock, Alexander was celebrating the victory with the chief of the tribe. His eyes fell upon Roxana, the chief's daughter and it is reported to have been love at first sight.

He was so taken by her that he made her his first wife by marrying her. It is said that he was truly happy and found a soul mate in her. His time with her is said to have been one of the happiest times in his short life. His queen bore him a son, Alexander IV Aegus. Neither she nor their son were allowed to survive however, and were killed by Alexander's successor Cassander in Macedonia.

Leadership Lessons of Alexander Great

Philanthropic Couples:

Bill and Melinda Gates - This couple has been very philanthropic. Bill Gates, it appears, has become a more generous donor to philanthropic causes after his marriage. He has used his wealth to aid many humanitarian causes, including a drive to limit the prevalence of malaria across the globe.

Mark Zuckerberg, the founder of Facebook and his wife, Priscilla Chan have given hundreds of millions of dollars to charitable causes and have pledged to give away half of their wealth during their lifetime.

Actionable points

1. If you find a person that you love, you should honor and cherish them A good supportive spouse can take you far. The converse also stands - a bad spouse makes for a steep fall in your fortunes. So be careful in the choice of who you decide to spend your life with.

2. Never stop believing in true love and act on it when you find it.

3. Let your compassion be greater than your anger, your gratitude greater than your regret. Keep your heart open to love.

How to Achieve Your Goals

Leadership Lessons of Alexander Great

Lesson: Take Security Seriously

Life of Alexander:

Alexander the Great was poisoned to death. He had developed a love of alcohol and state banquets were an ever-ready excuse to binge yet again. He had alienated and angered many of his senior generals and should have been more vigilant about what was offered to him in way of drink.

Gen. Antipater, his regent in Macedonia, had grown increasingly anxious after learning that one of the other senior generals, Parmenion and his son Philotus had been executed by Alexander. Philotus, an able general and son of the legendary Parmenion were falsely charged with conspiracy and withholding information about an assassination plot against Alexander. Philotus was tried in a kangaroo court and executed in a painful manner. The father, General Parmenion met death at the hand of assassins sent on racing camels to reach him before the news of the death of his son might reach him.

Parmenion was a Macedonian noble and a loyal general to King Phillip and Alexander. He had been the key in many victories and was a hero to the Macedonian army. His pitiable death led to a significant drop in morale of the serving Macedonian troops. The die at this point had been cast and even if there had been no conspirators before; these acts of brutality and disloyalty set the stage for real plots to kill Alexander.

It is felt that the alcoholism may have a significant factor leading to the decline in the leadership skills of Alexander the Great during the last three years of his life. He grew increasingly erratic and somewhat paranoid. Some say that he grew forlorn, sad and despondent after the death of many of his close confidantes. His drinking grew heavier and the banquets longer.

The poison that killed Alexander is said to have been brought to Babylon by the son of Antipater and was mixed into the ceremonial cup of wine at the state banquet. Shortly after Alexander raised the initial toast and as he drained his large cup, he fell ill. He experienced sharp pains in the abdomen and languished in his deathbed for several days before dying.

Modern Hazards

Many tourists are drugged and robbed in their hotels by charming friends that they find along the way. They usually offer them an open drink in which a sleep inducing agent has been added in order to rob them. Accidental overdoses and deaths have occurred in such cases.

Aleksandr Litvinenko, an exiled Russian political activist was killed in 2006 from toxic doses of polonium put in his food.

Actionable Points

1. If you are somebody important and if others stand to gain by your death: Be mindful of your security.
2. Live in a safer part of the city even if it is a smaller home.
3. Do not accept any open food from people that you do not trust or from someone you have just met.
4. Avoid needless danger. Take security precautions according the level of your need.

Leadership Lessons of Alexander Great

5. Don't create enemies needlessly. Treat others in a humane manner and respect their dignity even if you disagree.

Repeated Lesson: Be Democratic Whenever Possible

Alexander was brought up on the principles of democracy and open debate. He utilized the democratic process to allow others to feel empowered.

A good example of the successful use of these principles is the aftermath of the battle of Chimaeron wherein the Macedonian forces defeated the combined Greek forces.

Alexander and his father needed to decide the fate of Thebes, which was one of the principal rebel states. They invited the other city-states to weigh in on this matter. By including them, Alexander avoided further acrimony and hostility and solidified his support amongst the non-rebelling Greeks.

During his war camps, Alexander was democratic and invited his generals to present their strategies without fear of criticism. He frankly debated the merits of each case and was willing to relinquish his own opinion if a better reasoning for a course of action could be provided. This sense of democracy and participation motivated his generals to excel and contribute to making the common plan a success.

Take Away Points:

1. Invite ideas from your colleagues and subordinates. They should feel free to give their opinions without fear of critique or condemnation
2. Have an open door policy so that others are welcome to come and share ideas
3. Reward workers for volunteering good ideas
4. Be willing to modify your position if you are convinced that the course of action proposed by another makes more sense.

How to Achieve Your Goals

Lesson: Burn your Wagons

When Alexander the Great had conquered Darius at the battle of Gaugamela, and after his consolidation of power, he headed east for further conquests of the remaining lands. The supply train for his army however was made heavy with treasures that his men had gathered and progress became slower than expected. Alexander saw the problem for what it was and giving priority to his need for conquests, he set his own wagon ablaze. He then asked every man to do the same and they all obeyed.

He made a rousing speech about their mission, including the capture of rebel leader Bessus and troops who had laid claim to the Persian throne. Seeing the light of his reason, the rebels renewed their spirits and with their burdens lightened, marched ahead and pursued Bessus at top speed. They ultimately captured him and with his execution for the murder of Darius, they eliminated the last remnants of resistance to their rule.

They could not have done this if they had not unburdened themselves from their wagons. They made a temporary sacrifice for a more worthy long-term gain.

Modern Day Examples:

The Jesuit Priests:
The vows of poverty of Jesuit priests have given them a light drag and travel happy feet. They have a tremendous ability to take risks, innovate and settle in the remotest parts of the globe. They have served as beacons of learning and advanced the cause of learning while earning a good name for the Catholic faith. Their single-minded devotion and creativity has led to astonishing successes. They are so renowned for their abilities to achieve their goals that Kings have feared them and have had them banned by the Vatican at one point in history. They have also earned the moniker "God's Marines" for their ability to master any difficult situation that may arise and for being fearless moral warriors when the need arises. They have fought on the side of the have-nots, much to the consternation of colonizing empires

How to Achieve Your Goals

that wanted to subjugate and exploit the natives.

Their ability to lighten their load, let go of the past and blend in has allowed them to understand and empathize with people of different lands. Some rulers have been so impressed by them that they have been appointed to high posts in recognition of their abilities.

Steve Jobs:
The second coming is also a good example of someone who was not impeded by the drag of a wagon, i.e, the immediate need for financial security or reward. Steve Jobs led by passion and this got him into administrative battles. At one point, he was let go from his executive position at Apple, a company he had helped to establish.

He did not despair however, and went on to Pixar and made it a success. Without him, Apple floundered and he was invited back. He was the same Steve Jobs with his passion as great as ever. He gathered a world class team and produced a series of amazing products such as the iPod, iPhone, iPad, iMac and set up the iTunes industry that has taken the world by storm. He jettisoned any previous mindsets and beliefs that stood in the way of creative thought and collaboration.

Leadership Lessons of Alexander Great

Actionable Steps:

1. Do not be afraid of poverty; consider it your strong wall of strength. When you are comfortable with it, you are willing to take immense risks and will do whatever it takes to succeed.
2. Follow your passion, even when the immediate reward is not there.
3. Cultivate simplicity and moderation. The ability to lighten oneself from unnecessary requirements can give you great power and versatility as you move forward to your goals.
4. Look at what is holding you back. For most people it is the need to pay bills. See if you can cut back on your bills to allow you more freedom to innovate and take risks.
5. Be creative and seek a job that will be conducive to your long-term goals.

How to Achieve Your Goals

Lesson: Multitask Intelligently

As the vastness of Alexander's empire grew, the number of his war-injured veterans began to increase. He needed to make a disposition of the wounded, the sick and the retiring veterans. He also had an acute need to govern these far-flung areas using individuals he could trust.

He brilliantly met both these needs by setting up new cities at key strategic sites. He furthermore chose his worthy veterans to become governors and administrators of these areas and gave the less qualified veterans jobs under them. In this way, he could keep a strategic presence in key areas of his empire and was able to reward his decorated and proven veterans.

Modern Day Examples:
1. Even now days, veterans are given preference in certain job categories because of the type of training they have received. This makes use of their special training and talents while lowering the emotional and financial

problems associated with unemployed veterans. It also elevates the morale of fighting troops when they see retired soldiers treated well.

2. Provide work and job skills training for residents committed to correctional facilities. This allows them to develop job skills they can use later, helps to bring some income to the prisoners. It can also help the state defray some of the operational costs and can benefit the local economy. The decreased recidivism due to job skills and employment also lessens crime and violence in society.
3. Occupational training and education for prisoners: The education of prisoners and giving them occupational skills helps to keep them occupied while also reducing their recidivism rate. Good occupational skills also teach them responsibility and commitment which are important character traits that will serve them well in the long run.
4. The habitat for humanity initiative under President Carter serves to build homes for the homeless and also provides jobs
5. Promoting the education of girls in third world countries prevents their subjugation and abuse. It also helps the lower the population growth rate.

Actionable Steps:

How to Achieve Your Goals

1. Whenever possible, make a studied effort to target two or more goals together to get more mileage out of your efforts.

Lesson: Master Logistics and Organization

Alexander was a master of planning and no detail was too minor for him to consider. He is said to have declared, "My enemies may have more troops, but no one will be better prepared than me".

His troops were always well supplied on most campaigns. He timed the arrival of his troops to coincide with the harvest season when he could obtain supplies from the fresh harvests. During long marches, his forward troops would stock his areas of encampment in good time with food, water and other necessities.

He recognized before Napoleon Bonaparte that the army marches on its stomach. He never lost his supply lines and his army was often well supplied.

Many months before he was to cross over the Indus into India, he had the boats they would use disassembled and carried on mules and horseback for hundreds of miles to where they might be needed. Due to his attention to

How to Achieve Your Goals

detailed planning, his army was set up to succeed.

Modern Day Examples:

General Westmoreland was known for his logistical prowess during the Vietnam War. Many of the US battle victories were won due to his masterful orchestration of supplies for his troops. The fact that the war was lost is a subject for a different discussion.

Field Marshals Irwin Rommel and Montgomery both paid great attention to logistics and this is felt to be a key factor in the successes that they enjoyed. Ultimately, Montgomery, with the better logistical support was able to overcome his foe in the desert war and secure North Africa for the allies.

Actionable Steps

1. Make a list of the important supplies and resources needed to complete a task.
2. Arrange to have these supplies available.
3. Expect interruptions and distractions and have backup plans to ensure that work towards achieving goals is not affected.

Leadership Lessons of Alexander Great

Lesson: Timing is Everything

Alexander always chose the time and place for his battles and took the initiative whenever he could.

He would allow intangibles such as time, weather or a harvest season to turn the strategy of the foe to his advantage. He devised feints and baits to draw out the enemy from his prearranged formations in order to disrupt the best-laid plans. He also found ways to turn the strength of the enemy into a liability and used different ways to exploit it.

An example of this during the battle with Porus is the feigning of retreat by some of his troops in order to draw the opposing infantry forward from their entrenched positions.

The result was that chariots got stuck and the long bowman were not able to set their bows effectively.

How to Achieve Your Goals

In the battle against Darius, he chose the hour of attack and kept his enemies waiting all night. He did this for two successive nights and many of the opposing troops were sleep deprived and tired.

In the meantime, his troops rested and were at their prime when the battle was launched in the morning. At the battle of Granicus, he chose the time that positioned the setting sun to be in the eyes of his enemy.

At the battle of Gaugamela, his general Parmenion advised a night attack so that the Macedonian troops would not be discouraged by the sight of the large numbers of the enemy. Alexander's response, " I will not steal my victory like a common thief in the night" has been memorialized for posterity. This dramatic display of youthful bravado however belied the subtle and well thought out strategy he had devised to deprive the enemy of sleep by keeping them awake at night. He more than anyone else recognized that Parmenion had echoed the thoughts of Darius.

It was to his benefit to keep the enemy sleep deprived, expecting a night attack.

Leadership Lessons of Alexander Great

He also wanted to engage in the battle during the day in order to make rapid adjustments as needed by having a good daylight view of the battlefield. His smaller numbers needed to rely on swift tactics and maneuverability to gain victory. As history later revealed, some key shifts in strategy were made to prevent his left flank from caving in. Alexander was able to rush reinforcements where needed.

When an opening presented itself for an approach towards the chariot of the Persian Emperor, he was able to make rapid shifts in direction and head boldly into the heart of the Persian formation, causing a lot of disarray and panic. The ensuing melee frightened Darius, causing him to flee for his life.

When the emperor took flight, the Persian troops also began to turn their back and in effect ceded the great Empire to Alexander.

The victory on this day made Alexander effectively the King of Asia and the Persian Empire saw its last sunset. By choosing his time, Alexander was able to use his strengths and diminish the advantage of his enemy in his numbers.

How to Achieve Your Goals

At the battle on the banks of the river Hydaspes (Jhelum), the army of King Porus was arrayed on the other side. Instead of wading his army over to the opposite bank where the enemy was encamped, Alexander decided to travel about 15 miles north and cross at a section of river that was not defended. He did this on a dark and rainy night when the noise of movement would be muffled. He chose a time and place that were to his advantage and this was an important factor in his victory.

Modern Day Examples:
The Allies in World War II gave the impression of leading the charge elsewhere but crossed over at Normandy to their advantage. Despite heavy causalities, they pushed through and won the war.

Actionable Steps:

1. Recognize your vulnerabilities and your strengths. Do not be tempted into engagement when emotions are running high, but chose the battles that you need to fight with a cool head.

2. Recognize if you are a night person or a morning person and the times of your peak

efficiency. Use these times for creative and important tasks.

3. Recognize also the strengths and vulnerabilities of your foe.

4. Keep this in mind when you are scheduling tasks for yourself or your team. You want to schedule the most difficult tasks at the time of your peak efficiency. This will help you achieve your goal more efficiently with a higher likelihood of success.

5. Once you define your goal, be relentless in the pursuit of it.

6. Tactfully and with planning, step around all distractions.

How to Achieve Your Goals

Lesson: Build Alliances

Alexander the Great made many worthy alliances throughout the years. He was a good judge of men and their value. When he encountered a worthy foe, he sought to use his talents to make him an ally.

He did this with some of the noble families of the Persian Empire and with King Porus, who had put up a valiant fight at the Indian border. He cultivated relationships with the mother of Darius. She grew fond of Alexander and accepted him as a son for some of the noble deeds he performed to honor her and the memory of past Persian emperors.

Leadership Lessons of Alexander Great

Her acceptance of Alexander helped the Persian Empire to come together under his leadership. He treated the wife of Darius and his daughters with decorum, and the honor customary to them as a royal family.

His overtures were accepted and he was later offered the hand of one of the daughters of Darius in marriage, which he accepted.

He also encouraged his soldiers to respect and marry the local daughters of nobility from the new parts of his empire. He was farsighted and wanted to create a new race that would be a bridge between the two cultures. He arranged by some accounts some 10,000 marriages of this nature.

This was a lasting legacy of Alexander and many people in the territories of the old Persian Empire still trace their roots back to Macedonia.

He recruited able soldiers from the lands he conquered and adopted their techniques when he found these to be worthy of war. When his soldiers were pestered by the guerilla tactics of the Bactrian horsemen, he made allies out of them by offering them service in his own army after they were conquered. He used them to form a light infantry wing that was used in the fight against Porus.

The mobility and the accuracy of these mounted bowmen were legendary. They were

How to Achieve Your Goals

instrumental in taking out key positions of the opposing army. They were also the ones that took out many of the mahouts or the elephant drivers. Without their drivers, the elephants were targeted by lances and spears hurled by his famous spear throwers, who aimed with deadly accuracy at the eyes, hooves and ears of the beasts. The elephants turned back and ran enraged in a disoriented state, trampling many of their own troops.

Actionable Plan
1. Recognize and introduce yourself to individuals that have interests and goals similar to yours.
2. You can build alliances with them so that you may pool your resources and your experiences.
3. Different members of the alliance bring their talents to the table and the group as whole can benefit from the ideas and strategies of the other.
4. Some have called this the Master Mind Group that has a shared goal that is kept secret from others.
5. Other alliances may take the form of membership in certain organizations, special interest groups or meetings in different cities.
6. Make an assessment of what you bring to the table and what you are willing to

provide and communicate this to your ally.
7. Also, have an understanding of your ally's strengths and a clear agreement about what is expected from each other.
8. Check in with your ally from time to time to encourage each other's progress.
9. Above all, be loyal and honest with them. The trust you earn and reputation that you have with an ally is very valuable and will come into use in future projects as well.
10. Having a useful ally can make a big difference when times are tough. A good ally can provide motivational support, encouragement and logistical support to help you achieve your goals.
11. Some social networking websites such as LinkedIn, Facebook and others may serve as a fertile ground for choosing allies.
12. A good ally can open up doors and make your goals more achievable.

Lesson: Honor your parents/forgive them for any wrongs and move on

Background:

Alexander's mother adored him. She cherished him and gave him an abundance of unconditional love. She nurtured his self-confidence and indomitable spirit that was so evident later on.

Alexander also had a supportive relationship with his father. King Phillip, his father was very proud of him and confident of his abilities. He was wise and not overly intrusive. He kept a watchful eye from a distance, and focused on providing Alexander with premier learning opportunities.

When Alexander wanted to tame Bucephaus, the wild stallion no one else could tame, his father allowed him to try his hand in spite of a strong fatherly instinct to protect his son and keep him out of harm's way.

Others have described the event with much eloquence. Alexander's father watched with abated breath as he approached the horse with a fearless stride. He took the reins of the animal and turned him towards the sun. Alexander was working on a theory that the horse was fearful of his own shadow. His theory proved to be right and the horse began to calm down. He patted and soothed the animal and when he was calm, in one quick leap sat astride the horse. He pulled the reins in gently and when the horse obeyed, he allowed it full reign and let him run. The king and the courtiers were amazed as he turned the wild horse around at the end of his run tame, manageable and responding to his commands.

By using his intelligence to tame the horse, Alexander was able to show that he was the leader in intellect as well as valor. This also earned him respect amongst the senior generals and noblemen that were a witness to this event.

In keeping with his role a good father, Phillip hired the eminent polymath and scholar Aristotle and commissioned him as Alexander's teacher. He provided Aristotle the compensation that he desired and in addition, he rebuilt the philosopher's hometown. King Phillip also restored freedom to all of the town's citizens.

How to Achieve Your Goals

In gratitude, Aristotle worked extra hard to provide a truly world-class education to young Alexander and the other students at his school.

Alexander recognized all that his father had done for him. He recognized all the dreams that his mother had seen for him. He was grateful and showed his respect and gratitude through different ways.

He had his father's assassin killed and hunted down the conspirators. The prospect of his father's murderers escaping justice bothered him for a long time and he sought the counsel of the oracle of Siwa in Egypt years later in an attempt to ascertain this. Good oracles were considered to have such abilities in those days.

He also honored his mother by providing her the status of being the Queen Mother with all the power and privileges of that office when he went on his conquests. He wrote to her from the battlefield and sent her many mementos from his conquests.

Some women were seen as divine beings by Alexander. The idea of motherhood was so cherished by him that he even honored the mother of his opponent Darius. He afforded all the privileges that were due to the mother of the King, and to the wife and the daughters of his vanquished foe. He executed several soldiers that he found out had raped enemy women.

Leadership Lessons of Alexander Great

Thus, we see that Alexander the Great honored his parents and their love and in return provided him lasting inner strength. He always felt valued as a child and this healthy self-worth gave him inexhaustible stores of self-confidence.
Although he had some strong differences with his father, the fact that he was able to put this behind him was a factor that made him stronger as well.

Actionable Points:

1. Come to terms with your past.
2. Be grateful to your parents. Forgive the mistakes they made, if any.
3. Be grateful and forgive any abusers or tormentors from the past. By doing this, you unchain yourself from the negativity and are no longer influenced by their past or current criticisms.
4. Then, decide to take responsibility for your life. This means taking responsibility for *everything* that occurs in your life.
5. Taking such responsibility, start to act and set goals for your life.
6. Believe what Alexander said about achievement.

How to Achieve Your Goals

"There is nothing impossible to him who will try"

Leadership Lessons of Alexander Great

Lesson: Plan for your succession

Alexander the Great did not plan well for a succession. He did marry Roxana who bore him a son. He also married the daughter of Darius and took another bride. As fate would have it however, none of his wives or children survived the fierce struggles for power that ensued upon his death on June 10, 323 BC; 40 days short of his 33rd birthday.

He could have established an heir earlier as advised by his ministers. He could have perhaps taken better care of his health. He should have done a better job with his security detail and the screening of his food and drink.

It is almost certain that he was poisoned by his own senior generals after they became afraid of his capricious and brutal punishments.

He should have perhaps recognized that the death of his second in command, Hephestian might have also been an assassination as he too, died suddenly after taking a meal.

Furthermore, he should have stipulated to his most able generals a plan of succession. After his death, there was much chaos and confusion leading to the breakup of his empire into feuding kingdoms.

How to Achieve Your Goals

Take Away Points:
1. Plan for your succession by recognizing talent, and selecting them for mentoring and training.
2. Give them responsibility so that they may learn how to lead and how to rule in your absence.
3. The goal and the vision that you cherish must be clearly communicated to them.

References

All of the following books are worthy reads on this topic.

1. Alexander the Great by Philip Freeman
2. Alexander the Great and His Empire: A short introduction by Pierre Brian
3. The Landmark Arrian by James Romm and Robert B Strassler
4. Alexander the Great by Peter Green
5. Alexander the Great by Robin Lane Fox
6. Conquest and Empire: The Reign of Alexander the Great by A. B. Bosworth
7. Alexander the Great: The Hunt for a New Past by Paul Cartledge
8. Alexander the Great's Art of Strategy by Partha Bose

Epilogue

At the end, it is useful to consider some words attributed to Alexander the Great. His haunting spirit echoes in these words for all posterity.

"It is the most slavish thing to luxuriate, the most noble thing to labor"

"There is nothing impossible to him who will try"

"I had rather excel others in knowledge of what is excellent, than in the extent of my power and dominion"

"An army of sheep led by a lion is more to be feared than an army of lions led by a sheep"

"I am not interested in the noble birth of the citizens or their racial origins. I classify them using one criterion: their virtue"

"Each moment free from fear makes a man immortal"

"It is better to believe in men too rashly, and regret, than believe too meanly. Men could be more than they are if they would try for it."

The End

How to Achieve Your Goals

www.ingramcontent.com/pod-product-compliance
Lightning Source LLC
Chambersburg PA
CBHW072157160426
43197CB00012B/2422